20 Easy Christmas Carols For Alto Sax Book 1

Big Note Sheet Music With Lettered Noteheads

Michael Shaw

Copyright © 2016 Michael Shaw. All rights reserved. Including the right to reproduce this book or portions thereof, in any form. No part of this text may be reproduced in any form without the express written permission of the author.

Music Arrangements. All Christmas Carol arrangements in this book by **Michael Shaw Copyright © 2016**

ISBN: 1537431463
ISBN-13: 978-1537431468

www.mikesmusicroom.co.uk

Contents

The First Noel	1
Deck The Halls	4
See Amid The Winter Snow	6
Hark The Herald Angels Sing	8
In The Bleak Midwinter	10
O Come All Ye Faithful	12
The Huron Carol	14
O Come O Come Emmanuel	16
Away In A Manger	18
The Wassail Song	20
I Saw Three Ships	22
O Little Town Of Bethlehem	24
The Wexford Carol	26
O Christmas Tree	28
Auld Lang Syne	30
Ding Dong Merrily On High	32
The Gloucestershire Wassail	34
God Rest Ye Merry Gentlemen	36
O Holy Night	38
Unto Us A Boy Is Born	42
About The Author	44

The First Noel

Traditional

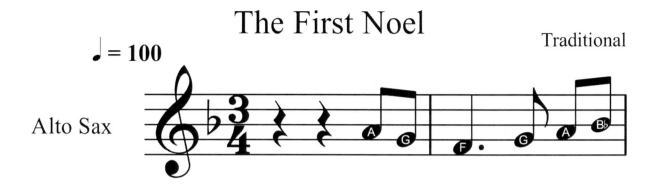
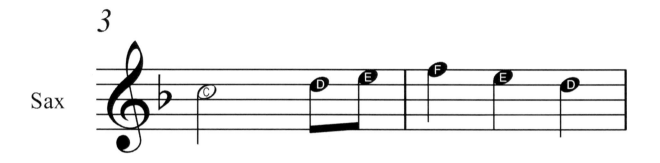
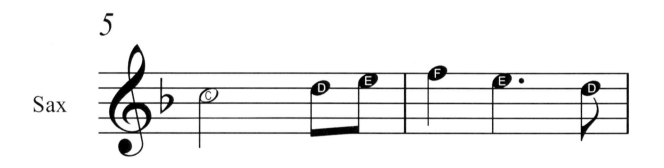
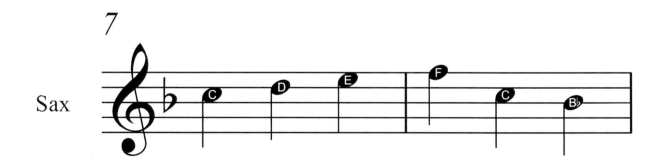

9
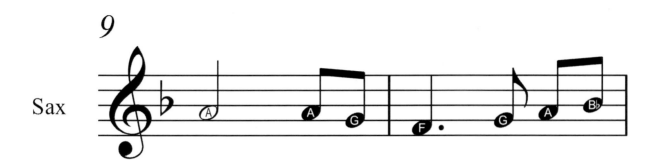

11
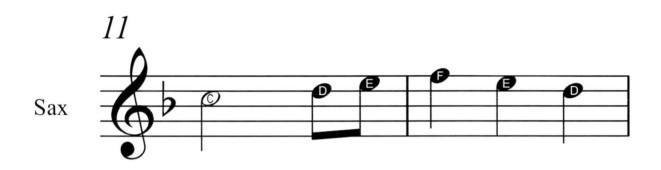

13
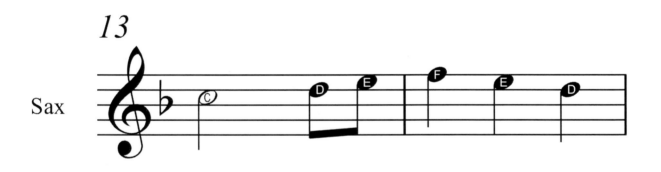

15
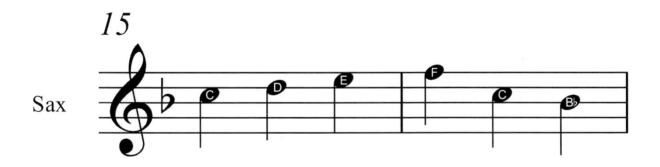

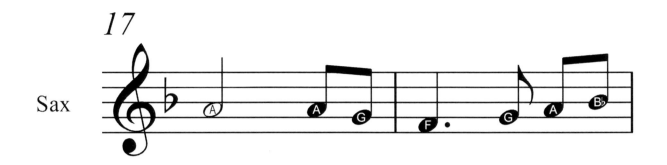
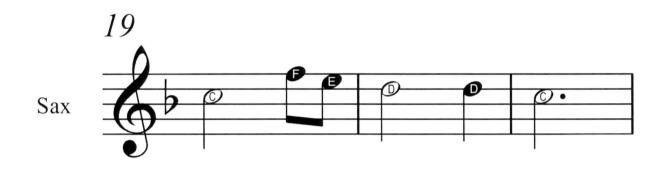
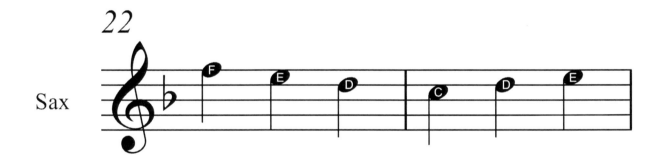
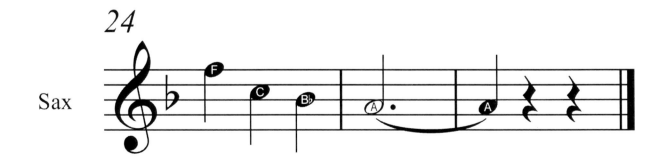

Deck The Halls

Traditional

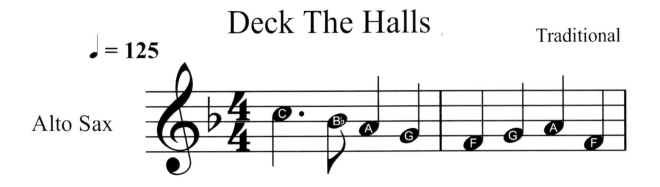
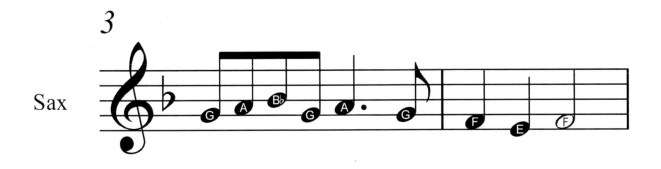
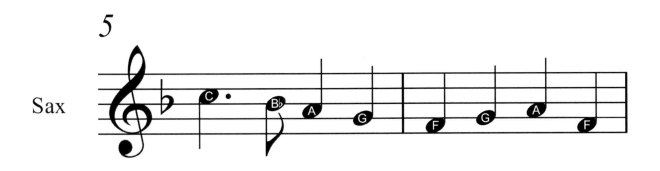
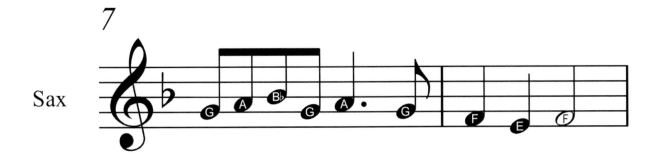

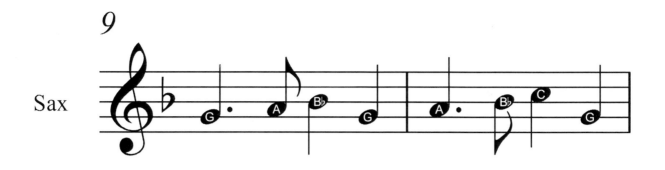
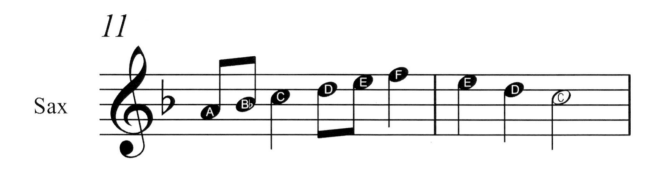
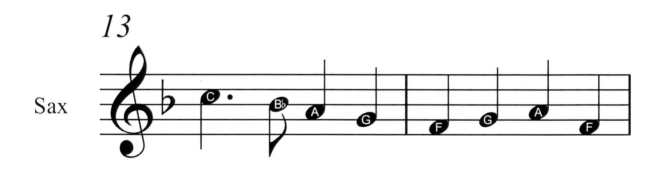
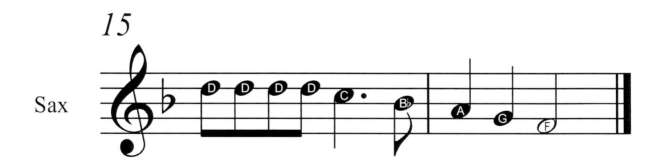

See Amid The Winter's Snow

John Goss

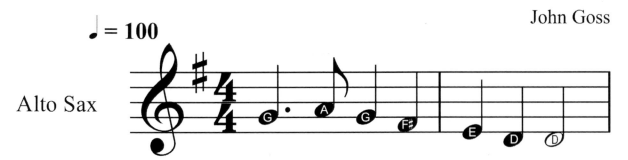

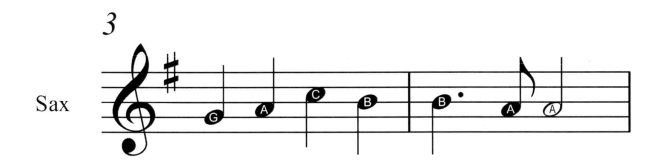

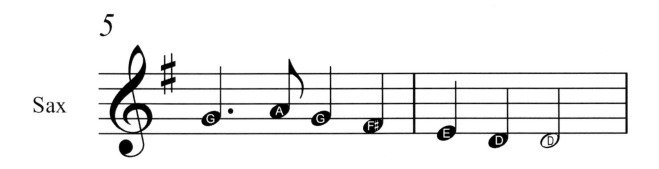

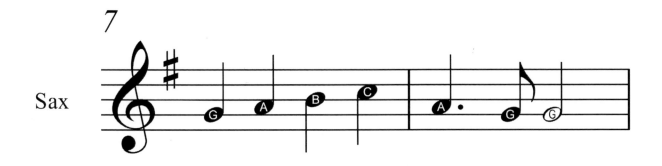

Hark The Herald Angels Sing

Mendelssohn

In The Bleak Midwinter

Gustav Holst

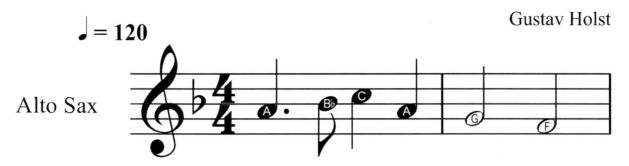
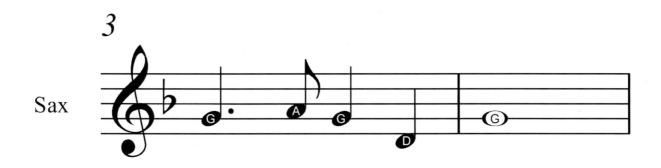
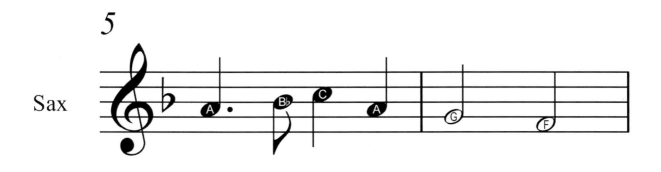

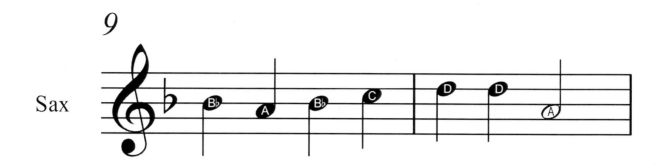

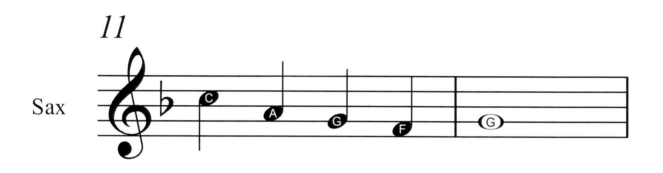

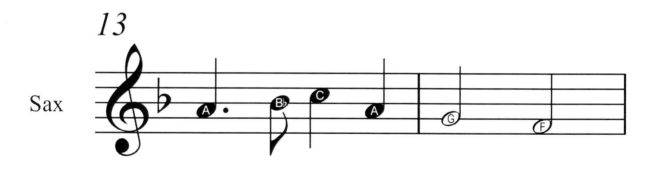

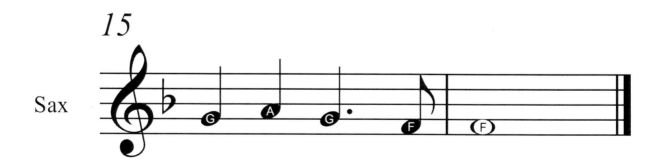

O Come All Ye Faithful

John Francis Wade

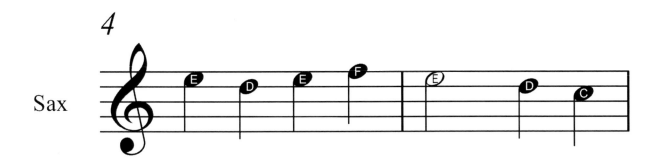

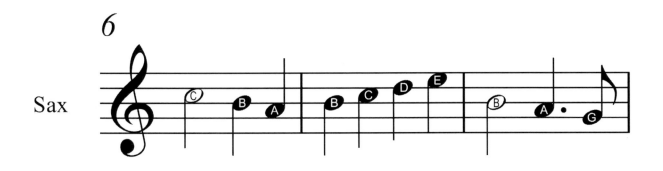

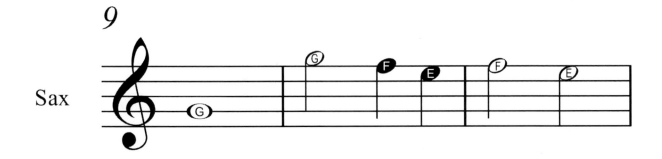

The Huron Carol

Traditional

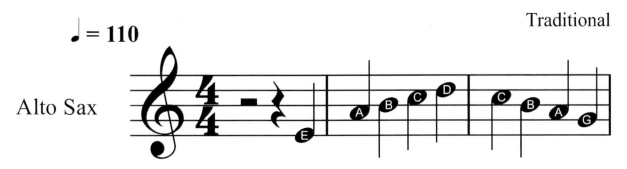
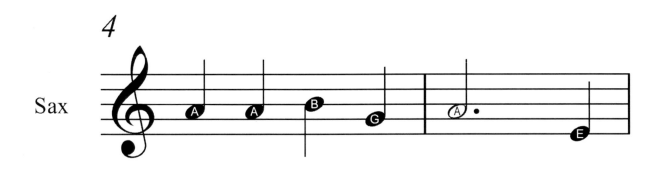
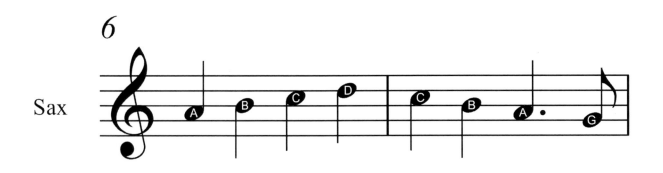
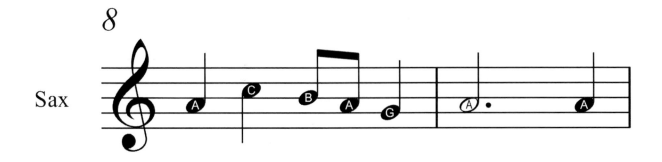

O Come O Come Emmanuel

French

Away In A Manger

Traditional

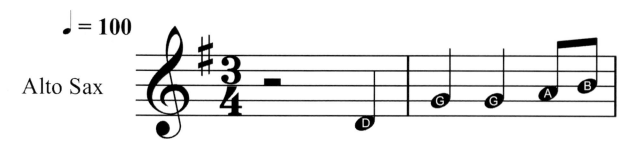
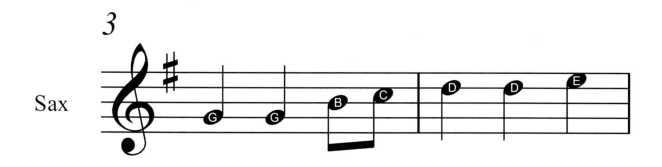
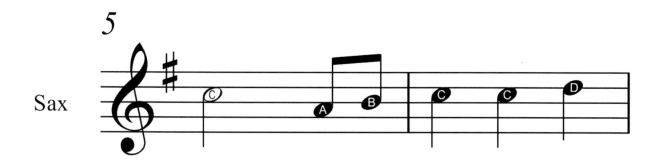
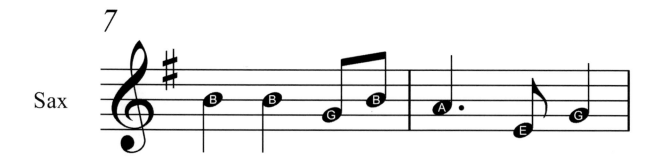

The Wassail Song

Traditional

♩ = 130

I Saw Three Ships

William Sandys

O Little Town Of Bethlehem

Traditional

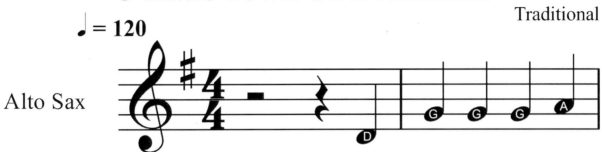

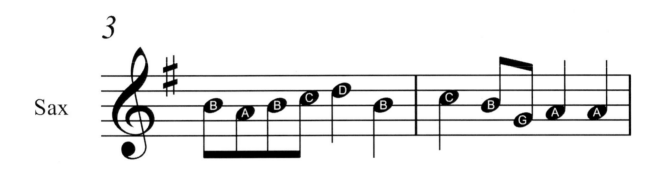

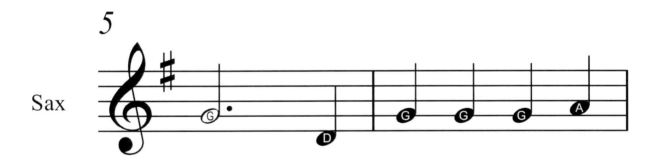

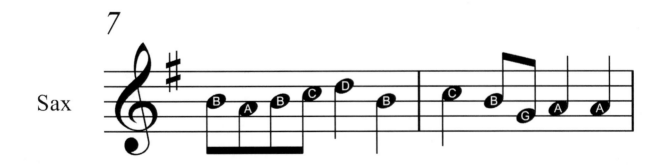

The Wexford Carol

Traditional

O Christmas Tree

German

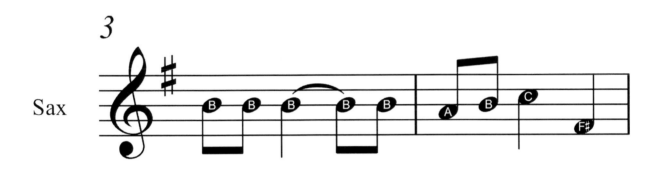
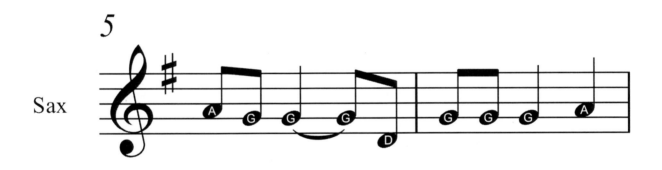
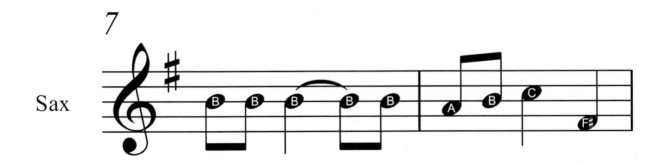

Auld Lang Syne

Scotland

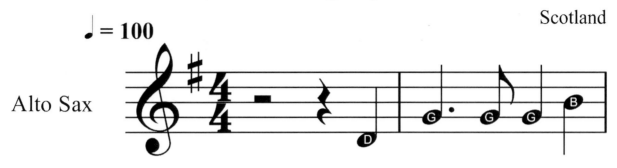
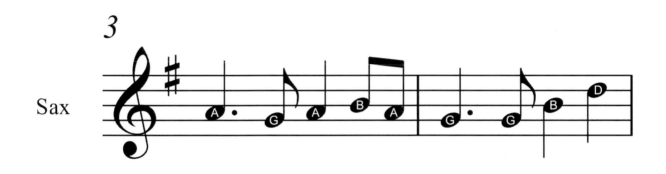
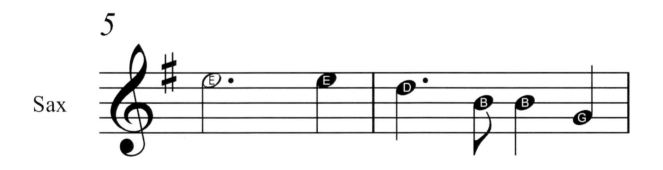
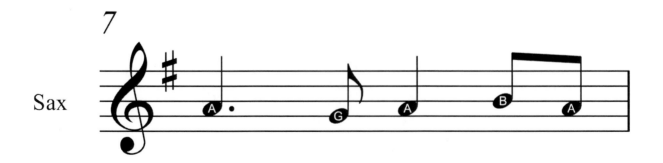

Ding Dong Merrily On High

French

The Gloucestershire Wassail

Traditional

♩ = 140

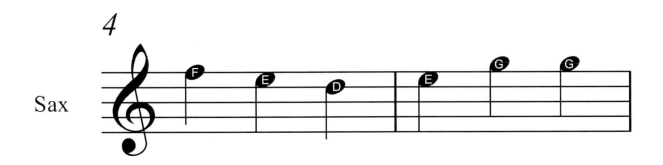
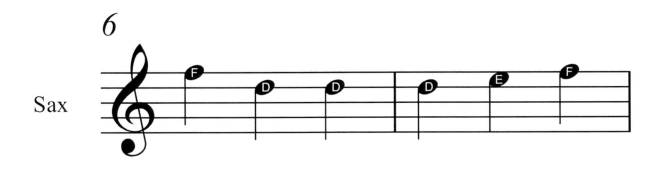
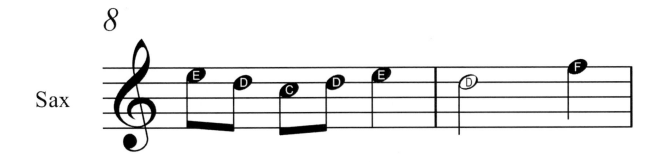

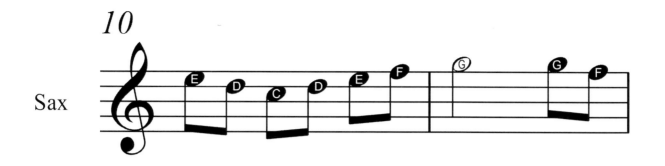
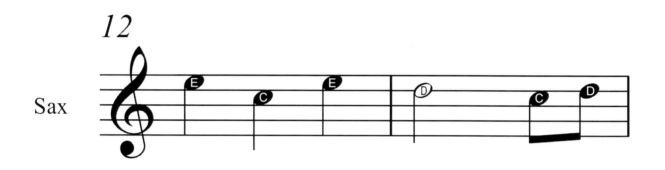
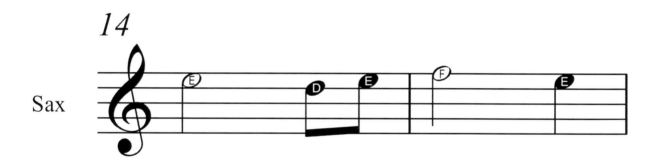
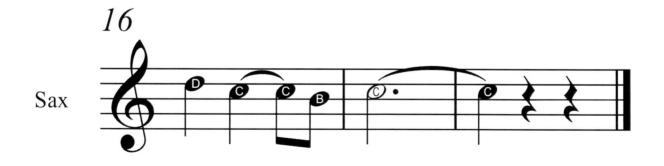

God Rest Ye Merry Gentlemen

Traditional

O Holy Night

Adolphe Adam

Unto Us A Boy Is Born

Traditional

About the Author

Mike works as a professional musician and keyboard music teacher. Mike has been teaching piano, electronic keyboard and electric organ for over thirty years and as a keyboard player worked in many night clubs and entertainment venues.

Mike has also branched out in to composing music and has written and recorded many new royalty free tracks which are used worldwide in TV, film and internet media applications. Mike is also proud of the fact that many of his students have gone on to be musicians, composers and teachers in their own right.

You can connect with Mike at:

Facebook
facebook.com/keyboardsheetmusic

Soundcloud
soundcloud.com/audiomichaeld

YouTube
youtube.com/user/pianolessonsguru

I hope this book has helped you with your music, if you have received value from it in any way, then please leave a review and encourage like minded musical instrument players around the world to keep playing music.

Thank You
Michael Shaw

Made in United States
North Haven, CT
08 July 2023